CONFESSIONS FROM A RECRUITER

CONFESSIONS FROM A RECRUITER

RESUME WRITING

David Janssen

ISBN-13: 9781523852512
ISBN-10: 1523852518
Library of Congress Control Number: 2016901958
CreateSpace Independent Publishing Platform
North Charleston, South Carolina

TABLE OF CONTENTS

INTRODUCTION

I HAVE SEEN thousands of resumes throughout the years, some were fantastic and others, well, we will just say they were less than desirable. We are all unique. Not all resumes are equal and not all employees perform the same. This book will not make you a better employee, however it will teach you some of the common resume errors, how to make a professional looking resume, and how to give your resume a fighting chance. For one reason or another, we have all found ourselves looking for a new job either by choice or by circumstance. It does not matter whether you are a victim of downsizing, have been laid off or are simply looking to make a change. If you are not prepared, this is an extremely stressful time. Truth be told, resume writing does not come naturally to most people. I've worked with candidates that had a resume professionally written, however, once they changed jobs did not know how to properly update it. This would often lead to inconsistencies, if they updated it themselves, or they would have to pay for another professionally written resume. I remember thinking *"if only they knew what recruiters were looking for."* That is the reason I chose to write *Confessions from a Recruiter – Resume Writing.* We surveyed over 100 Human Resource professionals to see what they look for in a resume. If you already have a good resume that is great, but you will find some tips here to make your resume better.

First, you need to understand everything a resume does. It serves several functions: to get an interview; to help structure the interview and serve as an interview outline; to be a reminder for the hiring manager once the interview is over; to act as a vessel for the manager to get feedback from other key personnel; and to substantiate a hiring decision. It is my hope that, after reading this book, you will not only feel confident in your abilities to write your resume, but proud to put it out for employers to see.

PART 1

GETTING STARTED

A RESUME IS usually the first—and typically the only—tool a hiring manager uses to determine if you are a viable candidate. Writing a resume can be both stressful and frustrating, however it really should not be. There are resume writing companies that will happily create a professional looking resume but it is going to cost you. Why pay one of these companies $100, $200 or more to do what you can do for yourself? I tried a resume writing company once and they sent me an extensive questionnaire to create my custom resume. I sent my responses back and they proceeded to ask for additional information. This process continued for over a month. The day finally came when I received my new resume. My excitement quickly vanished once I began reading it. It was nearly verbatim to the information I provided in the questionnaire. Obviously, the information should be what I provided but the only notable changes were structure and formatting. It is as if they took precisely what I gave and put it on my resume. Although it did look good, I couldn't help feeling I had wasted money and time paying someone else for the work I did. That day I realized I could have done this myself had I known some basic information about resume writing. The best thing that came out of this was learning the right technique for compiling data. My goal here is to give you all the information I learned so you can create a quality resume, feel confident about it, and maintain ownership of your professional career. I am not saying these companies do not provide good services, I'm sure most do; however, you can certainly do the same thing for yourself. This was a $200 lesson for me; you are getting this information plus a lot more for a lot less.

Your resume is something you "get out of what you put in", so take your time. The first thing to understand is that a resume is a living, organic document. That means your resume will, and should, be updated on a regular basis. This is true if you are entering the job market voluntarily, if you have been forced into it, or even if you are not considering a change. Job stability is never guaranteed. I have met countless people who thought they had seniority or thought they were too valuable and found themselves jobless. Trust this; if times get tough, an organization will do everything it can to survive. Have you ever heard of a CEO losing their job? Of course you have, it happens from Fortune 500 companies down to the smallest businesses. Losing your job is a difficult and an emotionally stressful time. You will find yourself asking questions like: *What do I do now? Did I save enough? How can I pay my bills? How do I support my family?* Do yourself a favor and be prepared. It is easier to remember what you did two or three months ago than it is to recall events from two to three years back. Review your resume often and update accomplishments, awards, certification, etc. This step is critical for peace of mind.

The second thing to remember is that <u>*you should tailor your resume to the position you are interested in*</u>. Let me clarify this; you need to be honest about your experience and never falsify information, but you are doing yourself an injustice if you try to provide all of your experiences in one document. There are two disadvantages to having an all-inclusive resume. First, this approach leaves you hoping you provided the decision maker with what he or she needs to know about you. This is like playing the game Pin the Tail on the Donkey. You are blindfolded, spun around and try to find the right spot for the tail. Most of the time you did not even come close to the donkey, let alone find the right spot. The same concept holds true here. You send in your blindfolded resume hoping it will hit the right spot. Just like in the game, sometimes you hit the right spot, but it was usually more by luck. We are trying to get you better odds. Yes, you do not know exactly what the hiring manager wants to see on your resume or what will even get them to move forward with an interview; however, the job description and job requirements are your

starting place. Look for keywords within the job description and requirement sections and make sure you have them on your resume. Typically,
resumes are sent electronically, which means whomever is reading it
will usually just look for keywords, hence it is important to have these
within your resume. For example, if a job requires experience operating
a forklift, experience with AutoCAD, etc. make sure that verbiage is on
your resume. Of course, only list it if you actually have the experience.
Remember, be honest! I have received countless resumes that had absolutely
nothing to do with the position the candidate applied for; those are the
first ones passed over. Most jobs have attention to details as a requirement. While you do not want to use that terminology on your resume
(more on that later) you can demonstrate it by ensuring your resume is
tailored to the job you are pursuing. *Note: If you are trying to change careers,
use a cover letter explaining your desire plus how your experiences make you a
viable candidate.*

The second issue with an all-inclusive resume is its length. Your
resume, depending on the position you are applying for, should be
between two and four pages with two being the preferred. If the last
page is not completely full, try to fill up at least half. Anything less than
that tends to look incomplete. This is merely a suggestion and is not
the rule. On the other end of the spectrum, I have received resumes
that were well over twenty pages. That is excessive. While the longer
resumes are thorough, hiring managers and recruiters will not spend
time reading them completely. Some may make a decision without reading past the first page. Hiring managers and recruiters usually take less
than thirty seconds, and sometimes less than ten, to decide if you are
a viable candidate. To illustrate this, go back and read this paragraph
again while timing yourself. Thirty seconds is not very long and keep
in mind a hiring manager typically has several resumes to review, not
to mention all the other things they do. Most managers oversee departments and they have deadlines, personnel issues, training requirements,
etc. so their time can be very limited.

PART 2

TYPES OF RESUME

THERE ARE MULTIPLE resume types but we are only going to focus on the two most common: *chronological and functional.* The chronological resume lists each job including the company name, job title, dates of employment and a comprehensive list of achievements for each individual employer. If you have lived in a variety of places, you should also include the location of each employment (city and state only). The list of jobs can start with the most recent and work backwards or vice versa. Although it is your choice, it is recommended that you begin your resume with your most recent or current employer, also known as reverse chronological. Starting your resume with your job from ten years ago does not give the best first impression. Remember, this could be your only opportunity to "wow" the decision maker.

The functional resume provides the same information but the formatting is different. With this resume, all of your accomplishments and/or responsibilities are grouped together and there is a separate section that lists all of your jobs, job titles, and dates in chronological order. I confess I do not recommend this type of resume. This resume is typically associated with little to no work experience (the candidate is trying to list a lot of experiences and accomplishments that are unrelated or non-specific) or suggests the candidate has low employment tenure. If an employer is looking for a specific skill, the functional resume will not indicate when or where you performed a specific task or how long it has been since you utilized it. Employers and decision makers want to see the details clearly and accurately. The last thing you want them to do is guess. *There are some notable exceptions to this rule. New graduates, those wishing to change careers, or who have been out of work for an extended amount of time might opt to use this format.*

An area that I see with the most inconsistency and unclear information is dates of employment. This information is used for a number of reasons and can lead to an otherwise good candidate being passed over during the initial resume review. A large percentage of the HR professionals we surveyed indicated that they review longevity (length of employment), the number of jobs a candidate has had, and employment gaps very closely. We will cover gaps later, for now we are going to identify some common structuring mistakes.

Always be consistent: if you use the month and year (January 2010 – May 2013) format then use that throughout the resume. Do not change the date format for other employments (4/2009 – 1/2010, 4/2009 – Jan/2010, or Apr/2009 to Jan/2010). I also see many inconsistencies when using the dash (-) or "to" in the dates (i.e. January 2010 – May 2013 versus January 2010 to May 2013). There is no specific rule as to which date structure to use, just be consistent. I feel that using the full month and year looks best but go with what you prefer. I also recommend using more than just a year structure (2010 – 2013 or 2010 to 2013) because it can be misleading. Let's say you worked at ABC Company from December 2009 to January 2010. If you use the year only structure then the dates are 2009 – 2010. That may look good on paper, however could mislead a manager into thinking you have worked at ABC Company for nearly two years when, in actuality, it was only two months. If this comes out during an interview or reference check (and it will come out) it can negatively influence the hiring decision or, worse yet, you could possibly lose the job if you are in a probationary period. On the other hand, think about a manager who has already had this happen. They may look at your resume and pass because they think you have only worked at ABC Company for a couple months when it was, in fact, nearly two years. Do not jeopardize an opportunity; give yourself an advantage by including the month and year. Here's another scenario, what happens if you worked at XYZ Company from June 2009 to October 2009 and use the year only structure (2009 – 2009 and I've also seen just 2009). In these examples, you should include a reason for leaving statement or identify which ones were temporary/seasonal work.

You should also avoid using exact dates (May 15, 2010 – October 12, 2014). It is hard to remember the exact dates for all employments, especially if you have had several. This can lead to inconsistent date formatting and, in my opinion, does not look as professional as just the month and year. *Note: If you have long tenure (three years or more) for each employer then feel free to use the year only (2007 – 2010) just make sure you can do this for all employers. Remember, consistency is key.*

PART 3

THE FORMAT

OVER NINETY PERCENT of the HR professionals we surveyed prefer a straightforward resume without fancy font themes, font sizing, or creative formatting. Keep it simple and let your background speak for you. Another reason to stick with simple resume formatting is for Applicant Tracking Systems (ATS). If you have ever applied for a job through a corporate website, your resume was probably loaded into an ATS. The ATS searches for keywords, education levels, etc. on the resume. If your resume does pass the initial ATS screening then it goes to the manager, if not, the system rejects it. A resume with various different font themes, sizing, and inconsistent formatting can confuse an ATS because it will try to reformat it. The problem here is that certain parts of the resume could be omitted or the system may reject the resume outright. This can happen regardless of whether or not you are qualified for the job. You have countless font themes to choose from, but unless you are pursuing a graphic arts career, you should stick to one of the more common: Calibri, Times New Roman, or Garamond. I feel that Calibri style looks best. The font size should be between eleven and fourteen, with twelve being the ideal size for the body and the larger font for section titles on your resume (such as Summary or Work Experience). Do not use smaller font because it can make reading the resume difficult and lead to a rejection. There are a few key things your resume should include: name, contact information, summary, skills or core competencies, work experience, education, and certifications. Notice that this list did not include objective statement or cover letters. We will cover those later. Check out Exhibit D at the end of this book where you will find ten different resume examples. I have been asked a number of times how to document multiple positions with the same employer. This can make a resume look confusing if not documented correctly. If you are in this kind of situation, check out Exhibit D example 4.

PART 4

SUMMARY AND VALUE STATEMENT

THE SUMMARY SECTION is your opportunity to highlight your professional career. Keep in mind that this is the first statement a hiring manager or recruiter will see so take your time. You can also use a value statement here, which is a combination of your summary and the value you bring to the organization. The big difference here is tailoring the value statement towards the specific position you are pursuing. Here are a few summary and value statement examples.

Summary Example 1:
More than 10 years' comprehensive experience in directing Human Resource functions, including recruitment and retention, conflict resolution, change management, labor relations and benefits administration. Adept in collaborating and consulting with senior management to develop Human Resources strategies and policies to support and further goals. Equally capable in business development and sales role. Team builder, capable of implementing best practices and motivating staff to peak performance. Utilize solid project management abilities to direct multiple priorities, and develop innovative strategies to meet and exceed performance objectives.

Summary Example 2:
Over 18 years' technical experience as a CAD professional. Proficient in the use and management of AutoCAD and its desktop modules for preparing Mechanical/Structural shop fabrication, and Civil

design drawings. Trained to use PDS, PDMS, & MicroStation with Geopak, and SmartPlant 3D. An accomplished professional with proven analytical abilities; excellent oral and written communication skills using Microsoft Office products.

Summary Example 3:
More than 8 years' performing a broad range of Accounting and Finance functions with strong emphasis on analytical, resolution and interpersonal communication skills. Strong team player experienced working cross-functional duties, along with multi-tasking and prioritization. Skilled in developing and implementing standardized policies and procedures. A proven hands-on problem solver with results in improving processes and diffusing difficult situations.

Value Statement Example 1
Offering more than 10 years' comprehensive experience in directing Human Resource functions, including recruitment and retention, conflict resolution, change management, labor relations and benefits administration. Adept in collaborating and consulting with senior management to develop Human Resources strategies and policies to support and further goals. Initiated new procedures that resulted in over 1,200 new leads obtained. Team builder capable of implementing best practices and motivating staff to peak performance, instrumental in coaching team member who earned top recruiter in the nation. Utilize solid project management abilities to direct multiple priorities, and develop innovative strategies to meet and exceed performance objectives.

Value Statement Example 2
Offering over 18 years' technical experience as a CAD professional. Proficient in the use and management of AutoCAD and

its desktop modules for preparing Mechanical/Structural shop fabrication, and Civil design drawings. Led the implementation and migration to new AutoCAD software. Trained to use PDS, PDMS, & MicroStation with Geopak, and SmartPlant 3D. Organization in-house expert and trainer; trained over 20 new personnel on AutoCAD procedures. An accomplished professional with proven analytical abilities; excellent oral and written communication skills using Microsoft Office products.

Value Statement Example 3
Offering more than 8 years' experience performing a broad range of Accounting and Finance functions with strong emphasis on analytical, resolution and interpersonal communication skills. Identified and corrected two quarters of P&L variations caused by spreadsheet formula errors. Strong team player experienced working cross-functional duties, along with multi-tasking and prioritization. Skilled in developing and implementing standardized policies and procedures. Developed new internal processes reducing month-end close out timeline. A proven hands-on problem solver with results in improving processes and diffusing difficult situations.

As you can see, the summary provides a clear overview about this candidate while the value statement is more specific with examples of your accomplishments. If you are struggling, use any of these as a starting point and make the necessary changes. Your summary or value statement may or may not look similar to one of these examples but you get an idea of what it should look like. It is specific and sets the stage for the resume.

Another mistake I see in a summary is tailoring the resume. If a position requires experience with a certain software, or specific work, etc., it is great to include that information within the summary but you also need to include it within the experience section. I have had managers tell me they like a candidate but what they were looking for is only in the summary. Managers are looking for key pieces of information (keywords) within your resume based on the job description and requirements. They also want to have an idea of when, how long, or how long it has been since you had that experience. We have all heard the saying, "you only get one chance to make a good first impression." That same philosophy holds true here. Once the manager makes their decision it is too late. Sending an updated resume will not change their decision about you.

PART 5

SKILLS (OR CORE COMPETENCIES)

THIS SECTION IS for you to provide specific details about your skills and competencies. Some examples include Change Management, Typing (50 WPM), OSHA Compliance, Business Development, Performance Management, and Process Improvement. **Note:** *This list is not all-inclusive and you will need to provide what is relevant to you.* Here are some different skill format examples.

Skill Example 1.

CORE COMPETENCIES

Strategic Business & Human Resources Planning & Leadership ♦ Policy Development ♦ Process Improvement Talent Management ♦ Performance Management ♦ Change Management ♦ OSHA | Regulatory Compliance Sales & Marketing ♦ Business Development ♦ Internet Marketing ♦ Social Media ¨ Finance & Accounting

Skill Example 2.
  Skills:

- Strong proficiency with Microsoft Office suite: Excel, Word, Word Perfect, PowerPoint, Outlook, etc.
- Virtual Meeting software such as GoToMeeting
- Adobe Acrobat Pro 9 and Adobe LiveCycle Designer
- InnoVest Systems, SEI and AMSI
- CRM, Salesforce and IAS
- Experienced with Microsoft Access, Crystal reports, Lotus Notes, Nitro, FBSI, Streetscape, Act 4.0, Publisher and Visio
- Type 55+ wpm
- Bilingual: Fluent English and Spanish

Skill Example 3.
  Skills:

- Policy Development
- Process Improvement
- Talent Management
- Performance Management
- Change Management
- Six Sigma
- OSHA | Regulatory Compliance
- Sales & Marketing
- Business Development
- Internet Marketing
- Social Media
- Finance & Accounting

There are skills you should avoid. Stay away from hard worker, good listener, fast learner, motivated, team player, honest, trustworthy, and attention to detail. The list could go on and on, but hopefully you see the problem here. These are too generic, subjective, and fluff.

PART 6

WORK EXPERIENCE

WORK EXPERIENCE IS the area you will want to review and tailor based on the position you are interested in. This is also the reason you should have more than one resume. Again, be honest and never falsify information; however, it is nearly impossible to list everything in detail encompassing your professional career. Tailoring simply refers to reviewing the job description or job requirements and comparing those to your current resume. HR professionals are reviewing your experiences to determine what you can offer a company should they hire you. If you have the desired experience or skillset, make sure it is on your resume or revise as needed. This, in my opinion, is an often-overlooked step that leads to most resume rejections. *Again, review the job description and desired/required experience and include the keywords within your resume.*

The formatting in this area is relatively simple: company name, job title, employment dates, and accomplishments. *Note: If you have lived in multiple cities, you should also include the location of each employment (city and state).* There is additional information you may choose to include here, perhaps a Reason for Leaving (RFL) statement, identifying the employments that are either temporary or contract, and specifying the industry you have worked in. If you have experience within a specific industry but it is not clear just by company name or job title, it is a good idea to include the industry type (Oil and Gas, Aggregates, Civil Engineering, etc.).

Examples

ABC Company – Aggregate Mining
Accountant

XYZ Company – Oil and Gas Exploration
Engineer II

ABC Company – DOT Bridge Construction
Project Manager

XYZ Company
Forklift Operator – **Contract**

ABC Company
Gift wrapper – **Temporary**

Employers and recruiters look at employment tenure closely. Let's face it; layoffs happen, work conflicts arise, and families have emergencies. The RFL is your opportunity to explain why you have had short tenures that were not due to being in a contract or temporary job.

RFL Examples

Reason for leaving: Family emergency, relocated to Florida.
Reason for leaving: Budgetary cuts, laid off.
Reason for leaving: Company lost contract; laid off due to low seniority.

PART 7

ACCOMPLISHMENTS AND SAMPLE OF RESUME QUESTIONS

EACH EMPLOYMENT ENTRY needs to include, either in a paragraph or bullet point format (bullet point format is preferred, we will discuss these in part eleven), a list of your accomplishments. I feel the best reading resumes have a short job description followed by a list of accomplishments in bullet point format. If you have access to your job description then use that to provide your responsibilities. If you do not have it, go to the internet and do a search based upon your job title. You should find plenty of information to get you going. Next will be your list of accomplishments. A large percentage of HR professionals we surveyed look for specific accomplishments and what sets you apart from the others. Below is a list of some generic questions to help document your accomplishments. It is important to understand that this list does not encompass all careers and there are literally countless questions you can create to quantify your work. Again, this is a basic list to get you started and could be used for every job you have had.

Resume Questions

1. What are/were my responsibilities?
2. Do/did I have any direct or indirect reports? If so, how many?
3. What kind of budget am/was I responsible for?
4. Have I eliminated any unnecessary company costs/processes? If so, what were the savings?
5. Have I earned any awards/recognitions? If so, what were they?

6. Have any of my direct reports earned any awards? If so, what were they?
7. What are/were my biggest contributions?
8. What accomplishment am I most proud of? Why?
9. How much new business did I bring in?
10. Did I complete my projects on time or early?
11. Was I responsible for training anyone? How many?
12. Did I have any special projects? What were the results?
13. What did I do better than my colleagues did?

It is important to note that there are terms/sections that you should avoid: Responsible for, Duties include, or Responsibilities. These are fluff and do not add value.

Example to avoid using:
Responsible for, or Duties include, Responsibilities:

- (List of Accomplishments)

At the end of the book, you will find Exhibit A with the above questions as a Job Accomplishment Questionnaire. Use one for each of your employments and simply begin answering the questions. Do not focus on structure, spelling, or grammar at this point. This is going to be a very rough draft and you want to have plenty of data to work with. You can edit your responses later so write down everything. Most importantly, be honest with yourself and your answers. The goal here is to start writing. Writer's block gets the best of all of us; and this is usually when people start turning to a resume writing company. That's fine if you want to do that but they are going to need the same information so you are most likely going to find yourself right back at this step.

PART 8

EDUCATION

Not everyone goes to college or technical training, some start and never finish, and others need to step away and finish later. That is life and it happens. There are a few things to remember when documenting your education though. It is a good idea to remove the year (or years) from each education entry. There are laws in place to prevent age discrimination, but let's face it, we are all human. Removing the date does not mean you are misrepresenting yourself, remember you can provide your total years of experience in the summary section. It does not matter if it takes you two, four, or seven years to complete a college degree. You may even work for several years and then get your college diploma. There are, however, exceptions when leaving the dates in is a good idea. For example, if you have a two-year gap in employment because you went back to college then I recommend leaving the dates. You could also use an employment RFL statement i.e. Reason for Leaving: Returned to college to complete degree or Reason for Leaving: Completed MBA program. It is also advisable to leave the date (month and year) for a new graduate with little to no work experience.

Education is an area where I see a lot of fluff. For example, ABC University (12 hours' general studies) or XYZ University - pursing degree or in progress. If you are pursuing a degree then you do want to list it; however, make sure you are actually pursing it. If you started college six, seven, or ten plus years ago and know that you are not going to complete the course then take it off the resume. Imagine this scenario: You are attending a job interview and they ask about pursing your degree. You do not want the awkward situation of explaining that you are not actually pursing the degree. This will completely change the rest of the interview; it might end right then. It is great that you want to take credit for what you have accomplished. You can still explain your educational background and plans during the interview. The difference here is the hiring manager's perception leading into the interview. If he or she thinks you have been going to school, there could be a perception that you are close to completion. If the degree is required, or at least near completion, imagine the sense of deception once it comes out that you are not actually going to school. There are exceptions to this rule; if some college is a requirement then you should list it. The key here is tailoring your resume accordingly based on the job description and experience requirements.

PART 9

CERTIFICATIONS

THIS SECTION GIVES you the opportunity to list your certifications and any licensing that you may have, e.g. CDL license. Feel free to list all of your certifications with the caveat that they really need to be relevant to the workplace. If your resume is on the long side, you can remove certification(s) that will not be applicable to a job you are pursuing and help conserve space. An example would be an Accounting & Finance professional that holds a CDL Class A from a previous career. The CDL does not provide any information as to the individual's accounting & finance abilities. This example may be farfetched but this same scenario could create concerns with the hiring manager regarding the candidate's intentions. Does the candidate want to be an accountant or CDL driver? The hiring manager may pass right over an otherwise qualified person. There are countless individuals looking for work, meaning there is already enough competition, so give yourself a fighting chance.

Examples of various certification and licensing.

CPA
PHR/SPHR
CPC
TWIC
HUET
Forklift

P.E.
EIT
Flood Plain
Payroll
H2S expires May 2014
CDL Class A expiration November 12, 2016

PART 10

COVER LETTERS AND OBJECTIVE STATEMENT

Cover Letters

I HAVE MIXED emotions regarding cover letters, primarily because they get the least amount of effort. It seems more companies are requiring a cover letter and not entertaining resumes without one, so it is your choice whether to include it or not. A small percentage of HR professionals we surveyed felt the cover letter made a difference in their perception of the candidate. The main use was reviewing communication and organization skills. If you are not sure, go ahead and include it; better safe than sorry. Most people miss the mark with cover letters because they are too generic. The cover letter should be specific and is your opportunity to elaborate on why you are the right candidate for a specific position, or if you are trying to change careers. If you are including a cover letter this could be the sole factor in whether they consider you a viable candidate, so take your time. See Exhibit B for a template and examples of various cover letters.

Objective Statements

The objective statement is the most widely misused and outdated part of the resume. Some of the most generic statements include:

1. Seeking employment in a [fill in the job title] position with the opportunity for continued professional growth.
2. To join a stable company where I can utilize my skills, learn further techniques, and have the opportunity for advancement.

3. Looking to join a stable company as a [job title not related to the job he or she is actually applying for] so I can contribute to the organization's success.
4. I am seeking a [job title] with [company].

If you are using one of these, or a variation of them, I am not trying to offend you but I hope you can see that nothing truly stands out with these. There is no "wow" factor. Most people want to join a stable company and contribute to its success. If you were reading these, would it move you to continue reading or move on to the next resume? Honestly, you would be better off leaving these objective statements off. Hiring managers and recruiters see hundreds of resumes. Yours needs to stand out and make them want to read more. So what does a quality objective statement look like? Let's take the first two examples above and revise them.

1. Seeking employment as a [fill in the job title] with the opportunity to continue building upon my ten years of [e.g. engineering, quality control, logistics] experience.
2. To join a stable company where I can utilize my skills in [e.g. engineering, quality control, logistics], continue expanding my skills, and have the opportunity to grow within the organization.

These still need work but the intention was to mirror the originals and illustrate how small changes can make a big impact. The revised statements are more specific and that is what you want.

PART 11

BULLET POINTS

BULLET POINTS ARE the heart and soul of your resume and your opportunity to brag about yourself and your accomplishments. If you used the Job Accomplishment Questions (Exhibit A) then this section is simplified. If you did not, please do yourself a favor and complete it now. Do not skip this step.

There are a few things to remember about bullet points. They should be short, hierarchical (most significant or impacting first), specific, and (for the most part) written in past tense. These points are describing what you have accomplished throughout your career, not what you are going to do. The ideal bullet point format is **action verb (see Exhibit C), accomplishment, and result**. It is important to note that not every point will contain an obvious or specified result.

Bullet Point Examples

- Guided recruiting staff in best practices, resulting in direct report recruiter ranking #1 of 72 recruiters due to training, leadership, and guidance, and revamped lead generation programs bringing in 1.2K new leads.
- Boosted overall division production, finishing the year at #2 out of 30 divisions nationwide.
- Obtained free advertising thus saving more than $3K in fees through effective negotiations.

If you find yourself wondering whether a bullet point is effective, or properly structured, you can implement the "so what" test. The test is straightforward. Read your bullet point and then ask so what? If the answer is obvious then you have a properly structured bullet point. If it not, you should redo it. Look at the second example above: Boosted overall division production, finishing the year at #2 out of 30 divisions nationwide. The *so what* is "finishing the year at #2 out of 30 divisions nationwide". Now apply the test to just the first portion "boosted overall division production". What is the so what? There is not one; the statement does not have a measureable factor, it is unfinished. Let's look at another example: Obtained free advertising thus saving more than $3K in fees through effective negations. The *so what* is "saving more than $3k in fees through effective negations". *You can also reverse the order starting with the result: Saved more than $3k by obtaining free advertising through the use of effective negotiations.*

PART 12

PERSONAL BRANDING

BRANDING STATEMENTS ARE gaining popularity and, if done right, can be very effective. If you choose to include one then it should be brief (no more than a sentence or two) and placed just below your contact information. You do not want to be redundant here so review your summary and adjust as necessary. *Note: You should not include an objective statement when using a branding statement.*

Branding Statement Examples

Example 1

Creative and innovative marketing professional with over seven years' experience managing national-level accounts.

Example 2

Detail-oriented accountant experienced in developing new and innovative processes streamlining organizational closeout procedures.

Just as a branding statement can be positive, you also need to be concerned with personal branding. Personal branding refers to the way you market yourself. You may never have your last name on the side of a building (or you may) but you do need to think about the other platforms where you are marketing yourself even if you do not realize it. I am talking about social media. Most people have some type of social media whether it is Facebook, Twitter, LinkedIn, or Instagram. You need to consider what you are posting because employers are looking at these to gain a better understanding of your personality and morals. While it may be fun to post your weekend party pictures, just remember a prospective employer might not think the same way about them. Make sure you have a good profile picture and set the other pictures to private. *Note: Employers have reviewed social media accounts of current employees so be mindful of that. Your reputation takes a lifetime to develop and a moment to ruin.*

You should also consider your email address and voicemail message. While your college nickname may sound cool, you do not want to have kegstand@xzy.com on your resume. There are plenty of free email providers. Do yourself a favor get and get an email address that is simple yet professional (something like your first.last name@gmail.com), even if it is just to use on your resume. The same holds true for setting up your voicemail. Keep it simple and professional: "Hi, this is David, I'm not able to take your call right now but please leave me your name and number and I'll call you back just as soon as I can. Thank you." Think about this from the employer's perspective. Employees are a reflection on the company. If you are going to use a work phone number or work cell then they are going to consider your phone etiquette too. Avoid, "You know what to do after the beep," or "Hello... Hello... Just kidding, I'm not here." These are announcements you do not want a prospective employer getting. I have said it before; perception is everything and competition for a job can be tough.

PART 13

COMMON ERRORS AND CORRECTIONS

MOST OF THESE topics have already been covered; however, you need to consider how important they are. Always review your resume for grammatical errors and spell check it. You should put your resume away for a few hours, or even a couple days, when reviewing so you can see it with "fresh eyes". You will be surprised at how many errors you find this way. Another good tip is to read your resume aloud and see how it flows. If it sounds bad to you imagine how it will sound to an employer. Typos and misspelled words look unprofessional. Most job requirements include attention to details and good communication skills. A resume riddled with misspellings does not convey that. You can have a friend, co-worker, or family member review your resume. Just be mindful that a friend or family member may not give you honest feedback, so make sure you remind them how important this is. There is also a website, www.fiverr.com, were you can find a number of people who will review your resume, provide suggestions or recommendations. The cost is usually minimal and turnaround time is quick. If you are still struggling to write your resume, or just do not want to write it yourself, you can find reasonably priced writers there too.

Avoid including personal information such as gender, race, age, place of birth, height, weight, or marital status. You should also remove the names of supervisors, full employer street address and telephone numbers, a picture of yourself, salary information, and the phrase "References available on request" from your resume. I recommend not listing any references until asked, and then you should carefully select them. You need references who are familiar with your work abilities and have good communication skills. It is crucial that you let them know to expect a call. I often see friends or acquaintances who know nothing about the candidate's work history. Bad references will get you the same results as a bad resume or interview will, no job offers. Recruiters know that your references are busy too. A reference check phone call usually last about ten minutes, so let them know that. I had a reference ask me, "Are we almost done?" after just a couple questions. To make it worse, the answers were, "Yeah," and, "I think so." Unfortunately, this candidate did not get the job. The ideal reference is a former manager or supervisor. While they may not always be your first choice for whatever reason, they typically have the best insight into your work performance. If you are concerned, use a manager from a different department; just make sure it is someone who knows your work well.

As I previously mentioned, use a professional looking email. You can get a free Gmail email account in just a couple of minutes. Make sure your voicemail greeting is professional (make sure you do not have background music on your recorded announcement or music set as your ringtone. You should include any professional credentials (PhD, E.I.T., P.E., M.D., CPA, CPC, PHR, etc.) relevant to the job you are seeking. Use a mix of bold type, lowercase, and uppercase lettering; however, limit font size and font type to two variations (example: Calibri and Garamond style with font size 12 and 14). Be consistent with formatting and use bullet points, they are extremely reader-friendly. Quantify your accomplishments, hiring managers love seeing numbers that can validate work performance. Avoid underlining, it is distracting and makes your resume look cluttered. Avoid printing your resume on bright colored paper; stick with a lighter color on 24-pound paper. You can use regular printer paper; however, the heavier paper looks professional and makes your resume standout among the others. Only use commonly known acronyms and try to keep them to a minimum, this is especially important if you are trying to change careers or industries. Remember to include the industry (oil and gas, healthcare, etc.) for all employments that are not easy to identify.

Frequently Asked Questions

1. What are the styles of resumes and which is best?

There are four different resume types: Chronological, Functional, Combination, and Curriculum Vitae (CV). The most popular, and easiest to read, is the reverse chronological. The functional is associated with those trying to change careers, have limited work experience, short tenures, or recent graduates. The combination is a mixture of both chronological and functional. A CV is usually longer than a typical resume and is most commonly used by engineers, lawyers, scientists and other similar professionals.

2. What is the best way to edit and proofread my resume?

If you just finished writing your resume, it is best to put it away and let it sit for at least a few hours. This will allow you to read it with fresh eyes and you will notice more grammar and spelling errors. By reading the resume aloud, you can pick up grammar problems and hear how the information flows. Friends, co-workers and family members can review it too. Be cautious though; friends and family may not give you an honest opinion. Check out www.fiverr.com too. This is great site where you can review an individual's feedback, their response time, and background. The cost is usually around $5.

3. What are keywords and how do I use them?

Keywords are specific words a hiring manager is looking for that are relevant to the job you are pursuing. Whether you post your resume to CareerBuilder, Monster, use a recruiter, or apply through a corporate website, your resume is in an electronic format. Hiring managers have the ability to do a keyword search for either a specific word or set of words. This is the main reason for reviewing the job description and requirements for each job you apply to and tailoring your resume accordingly. Again, be honest and do not lie about your experience.

4. What key information should I have on my resume?

You should have your contact information, summary, skills, work experience, education, and relevant certifications. Stay away from listing personal information such as date of birth, race, marital status, and hobbies. Leave references off until you get a request and skip the objective statement altogether.

5. How do hiring managers use my resume?
This is a great question. Hiring managers use your resume as justification when interviewing and hiring. They can get feedback from other leadership personnel; get an idea of your organization and communication skills; and substantiate the hiring decision.

6. Can I just list my job duties or responsibilities?
Yes, but you should not. The job market is tough; you want to provide your work accomplishments to help you stand out from the competition. Quantifiable accomplishments are ideal. Managers love seeing numbers. Compare these two: The top sales agent in the organization or; #1 out of 15 sales agent in the organization. The second one is quantifiable.

7. What is the biggest resume mistake?
The biggest mistake is sending a resume with grammatical errors, misspellings, inconsistent formatting, and vague details. This resume has your name on it and is probably the only thing a manager has on which to base a decision. You can only make one first impression, avoid the mistakes.

Final Thoughts
Whether you are new to resume writing or a seasoned professional, I hope that you found valuable information in this book. Writing a resume should not be overly stressful. Use the examples and questionnaire provided, take action, and do not get overwhelmed. You can find the examples from this book and other helpful resume tips at *www.confessionsfromarecruiter.com*. If you need further help, check out *www.fiverr.com* where you can find inexpensive professionals ready to help.

Send me an email to **david@confessionsfromarecruiter.com** and let me know what you loved or hated about the book. I can't promise I will respond to all emails, but it will certainly increase the probability if you tell me how helpful the information is and how you recommended it to all of your friends and coworkers. Word of mouth is a great asset, but, seriously, the job market changes often and so will the structure of a great resume. If there is something you wish had been included in the book, let me know and it might appear in future editions. Thank you for purchasing, I hope you found the information useful and the art of writing a resume less stressful.

Wishing you all prosperity and continued success.
David

Exhibit A.   **Job Accomplishment Questionnaire**

1. What are/were my responsibilities?

2. Did/do I have any direct or indirect reports?

3. What kind of budget am/was I responsible for?

4. Did I eliminate any unnecessary company cost/processes? If so, what were the savings?

5. Did I earn any awards/recognitions? If so, what were they?

6. Did any of my direct reports earn any awards? If so, what were they?

7. What are/were my biggest contributions?

8. What accomplishments am I most proud of?

9. How much new business do/did I bring in?

10. Do/Did I complete my projects on time or early?

11. Am/Was I responsible for training anyone? How many?

12. Did I have any special projects? What were the results?

13. What did I do better than my colleagues did?

Exhibit B, Example 1.   **Cover Letter Template/Examples**

[Name]
[Address]
[Phone Number]
[Email]

[Date]

Dear Hiring Manager or his or her name if known.
[The Company Name]

Re: The job title/position you are pursing.

I am interested in the [job title and location].

The following comparison of my skills and accomplishments to the requirements listed on the job description demonstrate the necessary education and experience.

Requirement – *Look within the job requirements and list the main require-ments, e.g. must have a specific education level/degree, must have specific expe-rience, must have experience with a specific software system or database. Try to list each requirement separately but you can group them if the requirements are similar in nature.*
Accomplishment –

- *Explain how you meet the requirement. You can take this response directly from your resume and simply paste it here but that is not recommended. Imagine if you were the manager reading the cover letter and seeing the same exact verbiage as the resume. This could be perceived as lacking communication skills, experience, or that you are not serious about this position. All of which are not desirable. It is <u>highly recommended</u> that you* *elaborate more on your accomplishment. This is your opportunity to get the hiring manager interested and "hungry" for more.*

Requirement – *List another job requirement that you can satisfy.*
Accomplishment –

- *Explain how you meet the requirement.*

Requirement – *List another job requirement that you can satisfy.*

- *Explain how you meet the requirement.*

I greatly appreciate your time and consideration. I look forward to further discussions. Thank you.

Sincerely,
[Name]

Exhibit B, Example 2.　　　　　**Cover Letter Template/Examples**

[Date]

To whom it may concern:

This letter is to present my professional qualifications and obtain a meeting with you to discuss the services I can provide to your organization as a(n) [Job Title].

I have a (just completed a degree or will complete my degree in two months) degree in [Degree] from [Name of University].

I have been working with [types of companies (example: engineering firms, accounting and finance)] for [years of experience] as a [Job Title]. During these years, I have acquired skills that would immediately allow me to be of benefit to your company.

Working as a [Job Title], I have had the opportunity to work with various disciplines such as: [Include job information and company details that are relevant to the job you are pursuing].

I feel that I can contribute to the success of [Company Name] and be an asset to the company.

I look forward to hearing from you. Thank you for your time and consideration.

Sincerely,
[Name]

Exhibit B, Example 3.   **Cover Letter Template/Examples**

[Date]

[Company Name]

[Reference Job Title]

I am interested in the job opportunity at [Company Name] as a [Job Title]. I believe my experience and attributes as an experienced [Job Title] can add value to your company.

I am a highly motivated team player with [Years of Experience] years of experience. In addition, I am proactive, resourceful and can effectively contribute to the success of your organization.

I am proficient in [keywords and task from the job description].

Thank you for your time and consideration. I look forward to hearing from you.
Please contact me at [Phone Number] or email at [Email address].

Sincerely,
[Name]

Exhibit B, Example 4.   **Cover Letter Template/Examples**

[Date]

Dear [Company or Human Resource members name if known] or Human Resource,

    This letter is to express my interest in the [Job Title] currently posted [Job Board or Company website]. From my [years of experience] with [Company Name] as a [Job Title], I believe I could exceed the company's expectations for the role.

    Through my experiences, I have acquired the skills that are crucial to fulfilling the responsibilities of the [Job Title] opening. One project that I am particularly proud of is [Project Name]. During this time I {List what you accomplished and how it correlates to the position you are applying to].

    I have had the opportunity to demonstrate exceptional communication skills. For example, I [provide examples of how you put out bulletins, held meetings, created meeting agendas, etc.] with clients regarding the status and progress of projects. Additionally, I led team trainings and mentored [number of co-workers, trainees] which allowing us to maintain the highest level of personnel resources and finish all projects on time and within budget.

    I am highly interested in this position and feel that I can contribute to [Company Name] successes. Please contact me through phone or email if you would like to discuss my qualifications. Thank you for your time and consideration. I look forward to hearing from you soon.

Sincerely,
[Name]

Exhibit B, Example 5.   **Cover Letter Template/Examples**

[Date]

Dear Human Resources,

My name is [Name]. I am a [Job Title] with [Years] years of professional experience. I am writing to express my interest in the [Job Title] currently available in your organization.

Through my professional career, I have had the opportunity to work as a [Job Title] where I was able to [List accomplishments and/or responsibilities that relate to the job you are applying to]. I am confident you will find my qualifications a good match for this position.

I possess excellent analytical skills and the ability to think critically to solve complex problems. I am also highly motivated, a hard worker and have a strong commitment to a team environment. I believe in teamwork and working to enhance an organization's performance and reputation.

Please find enclosed my resume for your review. I look forward to having the opportunity to meet with you and to learn more about your company.

Sincerely,
[Name]

Exhibit C.   **Sample Action Verbs**

Accelerated	Grouped	Programmed
Accomplished	Guided	Promoted
Achieved	Handled	Provided
Acquired	Held	Published
Adjusted	Highlighted	Purchased
Administrated	Identified	Questioned
Advised	Illustrated	Recommended
Aided	Implemented	Recorded
Allocated	Imposed	Recruited
Anticipated	Improved	Reduced
Approved	Increased	Regulated
Assembled	Influenced	Reinforced
Assisted	Initiated	Reported
Assured	Inspected	Represented
Awarded	Installed	Reproduced
Balanced	Instilled	Researched
Briefed	Instructed	Resolved
Brought	Introduced	Responded
Budgeted	Invented	Restored
Built	Inventoried	Retained
Calculated	Investigated	Retrieved
Categorized	Judged	Reviewed
Changed	Justified	Revised
Coached	Kept	Rewrote
Collaborated	Keynote	Saved
Collected	Lectured	Scheduled
Completed	Led	Searched
Conducted	Listened	Selected

Consolidated	Located	Served
Constructed	Maintained	Shaped
Defined	Managed	Shared
Delegated	Marketed	Showed
Delivered	Mastered	Simplified
Demonstrated	Measured	Solicited
Designed	Mediated	Solved
Developed	Modified	Specialized
Diagnosed	Molded	Specified
Directed	Monitored	Spoke
Discovered	Motivated	Started
Distributed	Negotiated	Stimulated
Documented	Observed	Studied
Educated	Obtained	Summarized
Effected	Operated	Supervised
Employed	Ordered	Supported
Endured	Organized	Surveyed
Established	Outlined	Targeted
Estimated	Oversaw	Taught
Evaluated	Participated	Tested
Exhibited	Perceived	Trained
Expanded	Performed	Translated
Experimented	Persuaded	Tutored
Facilitated	Planned	Updated
Filed	Predicted	Used
Forecasted	Prepared	Utilized
Formulated	Presented	Verified
Fostered	Presided	Visualized
Gained	Processed	Worked
Gathered	Produced	Wrote

[Name]
[Phone Number]
[Email Address]

SUMMARY OF QUALIFICATIONS

Over 10 years' experience providing professional administrative support to executives and upper management. Accomplished, self-motivated individual able to efficiently manage multiple priorities and manage workload effectively. Proven ability to meet deadlines on assigned objectives and goals. Possess excellent analytical and problem solving skills as well as teamwork, interpersonal and communication skills.

SKILLS

- Strong proficiency with Microsoft Office suite: Excel, Word, PowerPoint, Outlook
- Adobe Acrobat and Adobe LiveCycle Designer
- InnoVest Systems, SEI and AMSI
- CRM, Salesforce and IAS
- Type 70+ wpm

EDUCATION

- University 1
  Bachelor of Business Administration Degree

PROFESSIONAL EXPERIENCE

Company 1   January 2013 – Present
Executive Assistant

- Assisted President with the operational aspect of the business as well as personal matters

- Actively involved in the implementation of projects either by leading, delegating and/or assisting with respective project
- Proposed, wrote and reviewed company policy and procedures
- Prepared company internal financial reports
- Assisted with contract preparation, filing systems as well as tax filings

Company 2   September 2012 – January 2013
C – Level Administrative Assistant

- Provided clients with all required forms and documentation necessary to proceed with the investment recommendation(s) as provided by the advisor
- Processed client financial transactions such as trades, cash distributions, deposits, tax and tuition payments as well as account changes
- Researched and responded to questions from clients and related professionals via telephone, e-mail, written correspondence and in-person
- Scheduled client in office and out of office appointments, coordinated travel arrangements, monitored advisors' meeting schedules, organized meeting reports, materials and agendas

Company 3   April 2009 – September 2012
Administrative Assistant - **Contract**

- Created and maintained employee licensing and education database as required by company in order to comply with regulatory requirements
- Tracked and entered in company's database, applicable employees investments as required by the SEC
- Prepared all organizational SEC compliance documents
- Assisted with onboarding of ten new employees and ensured the timely completion of SEC licensing requirements
- Generated presentations, reports, spreadsheets and memoranda for executive and senior management meetings

Company 4   October 2005 – April 2009
Senior VP Executive Assistant

- Provided administrative support to the compliance and operations department; ensured compliance of all rules, guidelines, regulations and laws
- Maintained vendor contracts and created a risk matrix database to ensure compliance requirements
- Administrated and managed all organizational websites. Maintained, updated and created client profiles for accounts online
- Maintained the company's CRM. Administered CRM users and or teams/groups as needed and set user permissions
- Troubleshot and resolved issues that arose within our client accounting system, by auditing and testing system
- Audited files and prepared files for conversion ensuring accuracy for tax reporting purposes
- Created and updated company's forms in the intranet for internal and client use
- Set up training session for all employees ensuring all compliance with all continuing education requirements
- Administrated payment collection for estates, tax preparation, counseling, and miscellaneous services
- Ensured compliance of PTO program for Operations and Compliance department employees
- Researched and prepared letters, memorandums, management presentations, organizational charts, expense reports, travel arrangements, conference calls, filing, faxing, scanning, emailing, etc.

Exhibit D, Example 2

[Name]
[Phone Number]
[Email Address]

Summary:
Detail-oriented leader in the Oil and Gas industry, applying years of experience to produce high-value and low-cost performance in instrumentation & electrical design, project management, team leadership, business development, field engineering & operations, and facility installation inspections. Specialized in leading the electrical design effort and managing the project planning for the production of drawings, renderings, schematics, wiring diagrams, power distribution, lighting and grounding drawing packages, one-lines, conduit & cable schedules and plan drawings.

Software / Technical Experience:

- AutoCAD
- Hazmat
- UL 508A
- NEC
- NEMA
- IEEE
- SKM
- Voltage Switchgear, MCCs, VFDs and Motor Starters

Skills:

- Panel Design
- Project Management
- Project Coordination
- Workflow Optimization Communications
- Budget Control
- Revenue Savings

- Business Development
- Safety Improvements
- Compliance with Policy Enforcement
- Technical Initiatives

- Inventory Control
- Inventory Management
- Inspections

PROFESSIONAL EXPERIENCE
Company 1
Engineering Manager   March 2011 – Present

- Managed team of eight Electrical Engineers and Designers exceeding QA/QC expectations
- Coordinated meetings with multi-engineering discipline vendors to review latest technologies
- Provided project schedule and weekly project progress reports for client review
- Reviewed vendor project proposals and negotiated to ensure the contracts will meet and exceed the minimum requirements
- Developed PLC control system specifications and HMI graphics development for gas plants
- Responsible for managing both internal and external budgets
- Designed and developed electrical one-line diagrams, electrical plans, instrument and control panel wiring diagrams, cable and conduit schedules, control room layouts, and control system architecture diagrams
- Performed preliminary valve and actuator sizing and verified vendor actuator sizing data

Company 2
Engineer II   February 2008 – March 2011

- Manufactured Custom Process Control Systems from initial panel design to final training

- Design included components, preparation of schematic and assembly drawings, creation of Bills of Material (BOM), and documentation preparation
- Programmed control logic, configuration of HMI screens, testing, and de-bugging of completed panel assemblies
- Traveled to job site to complete commissioning: inspection of installation, configuration of instrumentation, testing & tuning of control systems, and training operators
- Scheduled meetings between vendors and customers, coordination of project requirements, engineering calculations as required for verification of design, and coordination of purchasing

Company 3
Engineer I   May 2004 – February 2008

- Responded to customer problems/questions
- Implemented new ideas into obtainable results
- Maintained quality and critical sensory information from equipment testing
- Troubleshot data systems/software, structural integrity, and other sensory equipment

EDUCATION

- University 1
  MS Electrical Engineering degree
- University 2
  BS Electrical Engineering degree

LICENSE

- PE - 2007
- EIT - 2002

Exhibit D, Example 3

[Name]
[Phone Number]
[Email Address]

SUMMARY

An innovated self-starter with extensive expertise in Network Engineering developed through education and experience. Experienced working in a fast-paced environment with the ability to think quickly, and successfully handle difficult situations in both an independent and team based environment. A dedicated, dependable, and technically skilled professional with strengths in problem solving, multitasking, and time management.

CERTIFICATIONS

- Cisco Certified Network Professional (CCNP) Routing and Switching
- Cisco Certified Network Associate (CCNA) Routing and Switching

EDUCATION

- University 1
  BS Computer Science

Hardware

- Cisco 6503, 6509, 4506
- Cisco ASR 1002
- Cisco ASA 55xx
- Cisco 800, 1800, 1900, 2800, 2900, 3800, 3900 series Routers
- Cisco 3850, 3750, 3120, 2960X, 2960S

- Nexus 5000
- Cisco 7942, 7960
- F5 Load Balancer
- DMVPN
- Cisco VPN 4.6, 5.0
- Cisco ACS, TACACS, Radius

PROFESSIONAL EXPERIENCE

Company 1   2009 – Present
Engineer II

- Designed, implemented, maintained, and supported Data Center and remote sites
- Led enterprise projects, including the planning and implementation of new offices brought on the WAN, circuit upgrades, and added backup circuits
- Oversaw the development of infrastructure, supporting 450 Wireless Access points, and over 325 remote devices
- Administered network compliance for over 700 remote sites, as well as critical applications that reside within core datacenters
- Controlled network security, firewall administration, access and perimeter control, vulnerability management, intrusion detection, and security monitoring
- Designed and supported the implementation of M&A under existing networks, and consolidate hosted applications and services to the primary datacenter
- Configured and supported infrastructure behind A12 load balancers
- Established and supported VPN Tunnels with external customer sites
- Strived for constant improvement by looking for enhancements in our network structure and configurations deployed throughout the enterprise

- Troubleshot and resolved network issues using Network Automation, Orion, and Netflow Analyzer
- Supported and maintained existing voice and data network infrastructure
- Worked with various IT groups for compliance to security standards and policies as needed
- Created and maintained detailed project plans, scope of work, and other technical documentation of all changes in the network
- Provided continuous research, assessment, and implementation of new technologies, hardware, and software needed to advance the applications and services rendered to the company
- Advanced support for employee remote access to the private network through VPN and Aruba remote access points

Company 2   2006 – 2009
Engineer I

- Application support specialist for 45 internal applications and websites for both affiliates and non-affiliates
- Setup and configured application websites on production servers, allowing for traffic over HTTP port 80 and HTTPS port 443
- Administered host files entries on application servers
- Implemented and updated new application on both Staging and Production servers
- Troubleshot issues and provided server maintenance on both testing and production servers
- Maintained a clustered terminal server environment and hosting application: troubleshot and resolved performance issues, network printing issues and software bugs within corporate terminal server environment
- Responsible for application enhancements, updating data, and break-fix through the execution of SQL Scripts on database servers

- Worked directly with developers, server, exchange, and database engineers to resolve issues and provide constant improvement
- Worked on call and performed after hours change requests to production systems
- Subject matter expert for the assigned business applications

Exhibit D, Example 4 *(Multiple positions with the same company)*

[Name]
[Phone Number]
[Email Address]

SUMMARY

Fleet Management professional offering over 15 years' proven success bringing independently operated companies to work together in achieving fiscal and operational goals. Goals achieved through gradual but strategic shift to centralization for leveraging purchase power, improving vendor performance and optimizing fleet utilization.

SKILLS

- Contract Negotiations
- Internal Audit
- Forecasting and Budgeting
- Fixed Asset compliance
- SEC Compliance
- Equipment acquisition

EXPERIENCE

Company 1   1999 – Present
Fleet Manager 2011 - Current
Fleet Manager

- Led collaborative effort to develop, implement and maintain policies and procedures related to fleet acquisition, utilization, maintenance and disposition for combined fleet of over 65,000 pieces of equipment with a budget of $850M
- Instrumental in the integration of new acquisitions
- Reviewed lease and capital expenditure forecast for each operating company

- Validated each subordinate company's budget through effective auditing procedures
- Monitored and approved all assets with cost exceeding certain thresholds prior to acquisition
- Initiated equipment standardization recommendations based on historical purchases, monthly forecasts and discussions with equipment managers and operations personnel
- Managed entire fleet and equipment assets relating to national agreements; monitored current agreements

Fleet Leader 2008 - 2011

- Conducted yearly planning, auditing, and recommendations of acquisition strategy; Lease vs. Buy vs. Rent
- Continually focused on equipment utilization through sharing and transferring of equipment
- Facilitated conference calls and email distribution for posting availability and required equipment needs, saving in excess of $1.5M
- Responsible for utilization of all remote equipment opportunities before approving dispositions
- Spearheaded environmental compliances requirement ensuring all equipment went through proper in service, preventative maintenance was adhered to OEM requirements and required inspections performed timely

Supply Chain Manager 2005 – 2008

- Managed organization's credit card program and negotiated monthly rebates with no card fees
- Trained fleet personnel and operations to share equipment related issues, concerns or improvements
- Provided key leadership skills cultivating relationships among fleet and operations personnel ensuring continuity and operational readiness

Supply Chain Lead 1999 - 2005

- Continual focus to be cost effective and efficient through fleet consistency
- Achieved aggressive pricing and timely dealer support by minimizing acquisition points
- Developed strategic partnerships, eliminating long lead times on key equipment: efforts saved millions, shortened lead times, reinforced standardization and minimized equipment rentals
- Led team integrating GPS technology throughout the fleet; efforts led to greater accountability and reduced costs associated with mileage, location, and utilization data
- Consistent communication with vendors and operations to confirm receipt and operational status of equipment

EDUCATION

- University 1
  MS Supply Chain Management degree
- University 2
  BS Fleet Management degree
- University 3
  BS Accounting degree

CERTIFICATIONS

- Six Sigma, Black Belt
- Asset Management
- Train the Trainer
- EEOC Compliance
- EPA Compliance

Exhibit D, Example 5

[Name]
[Phone Number]
[Email Address]
[Current City State]

SUMMARY

More than 10 years' comprehensive experience in directing Human Resource functions, including recruitment and retention, conflict resolution, change management, labor relations and benefits administration. Adept in collaborating and consulting with senior management to develop Human Resources strategies and policies to support and further goals. Equally capable in business development and sales role. Team builder, capable of implementing best practices and motivating staff to peak performance. Utilize solid project management abilities to direct multiple priorities, and develop innovative strategies to meet and exceed performance objectives. Recruiting experience includes a full spectrum of fields including Aircraft Mechanical Specialist, Aircraft Electronic Specialist, Law Enforcement, Medical Personnel, IT, Linguist, Dentist, etc.

CORE COMPETENCIES

- Strategic Business & Human Resources Planning & Leadership
- Policy Development
- Process Improvement
- Talent Management
- Performance Management

- Change Management

- OSHA | Regulatory Compliance
- Sales & Marketing
- Business Development
- Internet Marketing

WORK EXPERIENCE
Company 1   April 2012 – Present
Executive Recruiter

- Represented clients within a broad spectrum of industries including Oil & Gas, Food & Beverage, and Public Infrastructure
- Specialized in Accounting & Finance candidates in various types and levels of candidate
- Utilized a variety of techniques to fulfill client needs including direct recruiting, referrals, and use of social media
- Full cycle recruitment including prospecting, pre-screening, resume review and feedback, interview preparation, and compensation negotiation

Company 2   May 2010 – April 2012
Engineering Recruiter - **Contract**

- Represented clients in various business segments in the Oil & Gas Industry and Civil Engineer, Public & Private Infrastructure
- Specialized in recruiting various types and levels of candidates for clientele
- Full cycle recruitment included prospecting, pre-screening, resume reviews, and interview preparation and compensation negotiation
- Strong background in both the local and national onshore/offshore Oil & Gas market

Company 3   October 2008 – May 2010
Supervisor – Sales Manager

- Managed daily operations of 20-25 employees within a privately owned Oil and Gas Company

- Monitored daily operational procedures ensuring compliance with the Railroad Commission
- Assigned areas include South and East Texas with over $300M in operations assets
- Diversified professional, assisted with Business Development Team obtaining over $400K in new business

Company 4   June 2003 – October 2008

Director of Human Resources and Recruiting Operations

Directed recruiting efforts throughout Florida and southern Georgia. Diverse leader with eight assigned recruiters. Trained and motivated recruiters in four different recruiting programs. Assigned recruiting goals and ensured recruiters met or exceeded them while conducting market and performance analysis. Managed lead generation program. Developed and conducted recruiter training program employing best practices for new recruiting staff. Accountable for organization's compliance program to assure adherence to recruiting policies, proper document storage and disposal, vehicle usage and office safety. Managed nine-vehicle fleet and its $150K operating budget.

- Guided recruiting staff in best practices, resulting in assigned recruiter ranking #1 out of 45 recruiters due to training, leadership, and guidance, and increased lead generation program leads to 1.5K new leads
- Thoroughly vetted recruits leading to a 96% success rate; exceeded 75% standard
- Reduced operational expenses through effective screening of candidates
- Boosted overall production, finished the year at #2 out of 28 agencies nationwide

Company 5   September 2000 – June 2003
Recruiter

- Identified best practice that saved $74K+ in operational cost by eliminating screening deficiencies prior to applicant background screening
- Earned Light Industrial Recruiter of the Year award by placing over 400 candidates for CY 2002
- Avoided spend of money and operational processes by launching a tracking log and briefed staff in correct scheduling procedures; enforced scheduling regulations
- Achieved production rate 250% over assigned goal after selection to take over the Heavy Industrial Program
- Obtained free advertising, thus saving more than $2K in fees, by negotiating with local media outlets

EDUCATION

- University 1
  MBA; Human Resource Management concentration
- University 2
  Bachelor of Science, Human Resources Management

Exhibit D, Example 6

[Name]
[Phone Number]
[Email Address]

VALUE STATEMENT

Accounting and Finance Professional offering over five years' accounts payable/receivable experience with a background in customer service and account management. Strong team player experienced working cross-functional duties, along with multi-tasking and prioritization. Led team re-organization effort, saving over $125K in annual budget. Proven hands-on problem solver with results in improving processes and diffusing difficult situations.

SKILLS

- Microsoft Office, Great Plains, AS400, Data entry, Alpha-numeric
- Government contract compliance
- Vendor Maintenance, W-9
- Monthly Close
- Bank reconciliations
- Corporate Expense reporting
- SEC Compliance

PROFESSIONAL EXPERIENCE

Company 1   February 2010 – Present
Accounts Payable Clerk

- Managed Full-cycle Accounts Payables
- Coordinated organizational internal communication procedures
- Added new vendors to Enterprise system

- Created and maintained the payables filing system for each fiscal year
- Processed over 3000 monthly invoices
- Researched inquires and invoice discrepancies
- Routed processed invoices to corresponding departments for approval prior to payment

Company 2   September 2007 – February 2010
Accounts Payable Clerk II

- Processed 300+ invoices daily in Great Plains
- Cross-referenced all purchase orders to invoices prior to payment
- Verified the company credit card program ensuring transaction represents a valid expense
- Monitored, processed, and printed monthly checks, ran and manual checks as required
- Established Data entry and New vendor set up procedures
- Audited and analyzed internal discrepancies, researched and resolved past due invoices, verified monthly statements against company records and was the focal point for all vendor requests

Company 3   March 2006 – February 2007
Accounts Payable Coordinator - **Contract**

- Processed over 350 sub-contract and corporate invoices daily
- Streamlined vendor invoice discrepancies and created internal process to prevent future reoccurrences
- Entered and processed batches for payment for more than 1500 independent contractors per month
- Prepared monthly and quarterly payment requests for vendors
- Manually prepared expense requests for employees when requested
- Assisted with account reconciliation to the subsidiary ledger

- Accurately maintained a monthly accrual report for 200 remote sites
- Worked with internal audit teams and provided detailed information in daily tasks as well as policies, procedures, customer invoices received and payables

Company 4   August 2003 – March 2006
Accounts Receivable Specialist

- Completed detailed vetting process on delinquent clients by pulling credit reports, and DMV records
- Successfully collected and settled over 1K accounts
- Routinely contacted customers in regards to delinquent accounts to make payment arrangements
- Processed customer payments by obtaining personal banking information in securing payment
- Assisted customers with initial credit applications
- Maintained monthly and quarterly delinquent accounts list reducing overall delinquencies to less than 5%
- Prepared and sent monthly follow up letters to customers regarding current credit accounts

Company 5   December 2002 – August 2003
Management Accountant
Reason for Leaving: Company went out of business

- Maintained client files with current accurate information regarding operations
- Identified SEC non-compliance and created internal processes to prevent future violations
- Counseled leadership on benefits of reducing operations expenses, obtaining a more informed understanding of their current financial situation

EDUCATION

- University 1
  MBA, Business Management
  BS, Accounting

[Name]
[Email Address]
[Phone Number]

SUMMARY:
Professional Engineer with over 10 years' diverse experience. Experiences range from storm sewer design, drainage design, water and sanitary sewer design, to paving and grading design, structural analysis and design, structural modeling, hydraulic modeling, design of channel improvements, mooring systems, oceanic wave and payload research, and drilling vessel design. Strong leadership capabilities with experience leading research and development teams, monitoring timelines, and implementing creative measures to keep projects on schedule.

EDUCATION:

- University 1
  MS Ocean Engineering
- University 2
  BS Mechanical Engineering

EXPERIENCE
Company 1
Engineer II   March 2009 – April 2014

- Provided resource analysis for the Marques ocean current converter and wave energy converter

- Led the engineer mooring and stability Integrated Product Team meetings to develop an appropriate mooring design and dynamically stable platform for the San Carlos vessel
- Led project to characterize the resource of the Gulf of Mexico
- Analyzed operational budget, made recommendations for project budget, and scheduling framework

Company 2
Engineer Assistant   October 2006 – March 2009

- Analyzed ocean anchoring system used in Gulf of Mexico using OrcaFlex
- Reported simulation results to engineering team lead and research and develop team

Company 3
Engineer I – **Contract**   May 2005 – October 2006

- Developed numeric subsea model for Drilling Vessel utilizing electrical frequency for mooring needs

Company 4
Engineer II   October 2002 – May 2005

- Created Future Flow Projection and Future Scenario Analysis of Wastewater systems
- Recommendation of optimum solution for wastewater operation problem using InfoWorks CS Model & IPB Planning Tools (GIS & Excel Tools)
- Data Processing, Analysis and Use (Rainfall data, Wastewater Operation data etc.)
- Built Semi-automated Dynamic Excel and GIS Tools for data processing and analysis

Company 5
Engineer I   March 1999 – October 2002

- Calculated wind, earthquake, and service lateral and vertical loads using ASCE-7
- Designed reinforced concrete pedestals to uphold petroleum pipelines
- Designed and analyzed steel pipe supports and drilled piers. Used information from geotechnical reports to design industrial foundations

Company 6
Design Engineer   July 2006 – March 1999

- Designed drainage and utility layouts for future master-planned residential/commercial developments ranging from 25 to 200-acre tracts
- Executed an average of 65 projects from conceptual to final phase by collaborating with a team of three to five members
- Promoted effective communication among a diverse team consisting of different levels of management
- Utilized strong presentation skills by leading status meetings that ensured design quality and timeliness
- Executed engineering deliverables including project cost analyses, time budgets, specifications, contracts, and audit procedures

LICENSE

- Professional Engineer (P.E.)
- Engineer in Training (E.I.T.)

CERTIFICATIONS/ TRAINING

- Proficient with OrcaFlex Numeric Modeling Tool and Spreadsheet Software, Excel, ANSYS AQWA
- Coursework or some experience with AutoCAD, MATLAB, Visual Basic, ArcGIS
- Six Sigma, Green Belt
- ABS Certified
- HUET
- TWIC
- Rig Pass/Safe Gulf

Exhibit D, Example 8

[Name]
[Phone Number]
[Email Address]

SUMMARY:
Mechanical Engineer with 10+ years of Naval Architect design and vessel inspections. Strong background in ANSYS, FEA, power electronics & control system engineering, design, programming, and site commissioning. Adept at readily gathering and translating complex requirements into viable solutions. Record of accomplishment in interdepartmental collaboration, resulting in high-performance and cost-effective systems that are delivered according to specifications, within budget, and on time.

SKILLS

- Six Sigma
- ANSYS
- AutoCAD
- Microsoft Office
- Java
- Mathcad

- Solid Edge
- NEi Nastran
- Patran MSC Nastran
- Staad
- Solidworks

EDUCATION

- University 1
- BS Mechanical Engineering

EXPERIENCE

Company 1   March 2007 – Present
Senior Engineer

- Determined inspection cycles and life expectancy of systems and structures due to specific failure criterions
- Comprised direct analysis rules and regulation guides for QRT, steel and aluminum vessels, and both on- and offshore structures
- Assisted shipyards in handling dry-docking calculations
- Performed weld analysis
- Utilized Finite Element Analysis (FEA): Patran, ANSYS, Algor and FEMAP)
- Ensured designs meet applicable regulations proper classifications including:
- Cranes and Lifting Appliances
  o Mooring Systems
  o Naval Vessel Rules
  o Crane Barges
  o Underdeck Trolley Hoist System for High Speed Craft
  o Jack-up Rigs
  o Spud Barges
  o Bow and Azimuth thrusters
  o Rotating Equipment Vibration Analysis
  o Offshore Support Vessels

Company 2   October 2004 – March 2007
Lead Engineer

- Introduced Six Sigma processes; eliminated over 30% of the department's daily procedures
- Supported all phases of manufacturing
- Implemented Solid Modeling and increased use of Finite Element Analysis (FEA)

- Researched failure modes to determine reliability issues utilizing FMEA and historical data
- Developed cell specific drawings to avoid confusion on the shop floor
- Set interdepartmental procedures to improve information flow
- Worked carefully with the IT department to implement a new organizational ERP system
- Prepared the individual manufacturing facilities for internal and external audits
- Worked with Outside Inspectors hired by customers to ensure all requirements and issues were resolved
- Researched failure modes to determine reliability issues utilizing FMEA and historical data

Company 3   July 2002 – October 2004
Engineer III

- Designed and optimized new harness system to support high voltage power lines
- Developed portable substations to provide power in remote locations
- Performed FEA: Evaluated wind loads, seismic loads, and ice loads
- Analyzed buckling forces on steel structures
- Performed analysis on structure doors to ensure isolation and ability to withstand blast loads
- Researched and quoted materials and labor costs during the bidding process
- Determined foundation requirements necessary for soil specifications
- Organized databases of information to reduce research time spent locating previous designs and customer preferences

Company 4   May 2000 – July 2002
Senior Engineer

- Led the design and analysis of hulls, frames, and superstructure of DoD vessels
- Trained and mentored three junior engineers
- Inspected vessels for shock, vibration, and Blast Hardened bulkheads
- Designed structure in accordance with the DoD and civilian waterway policies
- Designed and analyzed corrugated structural bulkheads to replace corroded support brackets; efforts reduced cost and significant weight savings

Company 5   April 1999 – May 2000
Structural Engineer

- Completed structural analysis of DoD vessels
- Analyzed and redesigned hull structures to withstand vibration and shock
- Analyzed penetrations in hull, decks, beams, and bulkheads
- Performed Finite Element Analysis (DDAM, transient, thermal, dynamic, and static)
- Ensured designs met all DoD specifications

Exhibit D, Example 9

[Name]
[Email Address]
[Phone Number]

SUMMARY

A sincere, loyal and dedicated professional offering over ten years' warehouse and forklift operating experience. A known problem-solver with the ability to reduce downtime by troubleshooting, identifying defective parts and repairing equipment without costly equipment downtime.

WORK EXPERIENCE

Company 1   May 2008 – Present
Crane Operator

- Appointed Warehouse Safety Compliance; researched and updated 50+ out of date MSDS
- Regularly conducted workplace safety inspections ensuring OSHA production standards adherence
- Awarded the opportunity of bringing the Heavy Industrial Work environment into safety compliance
- Re-worked out of date spec parts, equipment, and procedures; reduced downtime by 25%

Company 2   January 2005 – May 2008
Forklift Operator

- Ensured shipment was intact and the correct bill was being delivered to the correct destination
- Inspected Packing Shipment, ensuring correct product delivery
- Completed 100% of daily and monthly assigned goals
- Detailed to oversee warehouse forklift operations and train new hires

- Monitored in-house safety procedures and enforced operating procedures

Company 3   June 2003 – January 2005
Logistic Technician

- Monitored and ensured compliance with OSHA production standards
- Offset warehouse personnel shortages; worked in the 25K Sq. Ft. warehouse as an order puller
- Developed internal Inventory Control procedures ensuring proper inventory levels
- Redefined and trained personnel on RF Scanner operation
- Created spreadsheets to track Lot number identification
- Maintained customer tickets during lifecycle of order
- Met deadlines on daily goals, often exceeding expectations

Company 4   April 2002 – June 2003
Warehouse Operator

- Attended daily pre-shift meetings maintaining continuity
- Ensured bill was being delivered to the correct destination
- Proficient in hitting goals on a daily and monthly basis
- Worked alongside supervisor to help get trailers out before deadline
- Ensured In-house safety procedures adherence; standardized operating procedures

Company 5   August 2000 – April 2002
Loaded and unloaded trailers

- Assisted with daily pre-shift meetings; kept leadership aware and ensured continuity

- Monitored packet slips to ensure packages were sent to the proper destinations
- Exceeded organizational goals; earned Top Warehouse Safety Employee of the Year
- Assigned additional responsibility of assistant shift-leader; trained new hires
- Monitored in-house safety procedures and tracked safety discrepancies until rectified

EDUCATION

- HS Diploma

LICENSE

- Class A CDL
- Forklift

CERTIFICATION

- HAZMAT
- H2S
- Confined Space
- Emergency Response Training
- Overhead Crane
- Forklift Safety
- Fire Extinguisher
- Two-Person Lift
- Safety Monitor

Exhibit D, Example 10

[Name]
[Email Address]
[Phone Number]

SUMMARY

Recent college graduate with an educational background in engineering with one year of industrial experience in the field of design and structural engineering. Expertise in working with CAD softwares like Auto CAD, Pro/E, solid works. Over two years' experience with specialized software like Fluent 12.0, ANSYS, ICEM CFD, MATLAB and PIV. Experienced in conducting wind tunnel experiments and handling PIV instruments, and conducting various high-speed flow experiments.

EDUCATION

- University 1
  Master of Science in Mechanical Engineering
- University 2
  Bachelor of Engineering in Mechanical Engineering (B.E)

SKILLS

- Computational Fluid Dynamics (ANSYS Fluent 12.0)
- Computer Aided Designing (Auto Cad, Pro/E, Solidworks)
- MATLAB, ICEM CFD, Gambit 2.4.6
- Finite Element Analysis (ANSYS), TecPlot 10
- XFOIL
- MathCAD
- Excel
- C and C++ Programming

EXPERIENCE
Company 1
Research Student   February 2009 - May 2011

- Thesis: Numerical Investigation of Hydrodynamic Focusing Phenomena in a Microflow Cyotmeter
- Performed Numerical Simulations studying the 2D Hydrodynamic focusing in a microfluidic device (cytometer)
- Performed Numerical study using ANSYS FLUENT12.0
- Studied Multiphase models such as Volume of Fluid model (VOF) and Discrete Phase Model (DPM)
- Developed User Defined Functions (UDF) in FLUENT to define the properties of the material and other purposes
- Studied the behavior of both Newtonian and non-Newtonian flows in the microfluidic device

Company 2
Engineer I   January 2006 – February 2009

- Developed Production techniques in the production of Structural works, Jaw crusher, Chemical Storage Tanks
- Used Pro/E, Solidworks extensively to generate CAD drawings
- Performed structural and Thermal analysis using Finite Element Analysis (FEA) software packages such as ANSYS
- Preparation of various important reports for submission to top management on daily, weekly & monthly basis

Company 3
Research Assistant   May 2003 - January 2006

- Planned, set up, and instructed laboratory methods and helped students in their projects

- Helped students learn to use different systems in the lab like wind tunnel, CFD software, PIV systems

Company 4
Teaching Assistant   March 2002 - January 2003

- Assisted professor in teaching 'Compressible Fluid Flows' and 'Thermodynamics' case study
- Tutored students by answering questions and explaining concepts during office hours
- Played a significant role in lecturing, tutoring and proctoring, grading and mentoring students in the course

Company 5
Engineering Intern   May 2000 - March 2002

- Developed CNC Parametric Part Program for machining specialized parts on FANUC 15M by 5-Axis CNC Machine
- Developed a new, innovative application optimizing the cost involved in order processing
- Manufactured blades for a steam turbine, maintaining efficiency and reducing the time of manufacturing

David Janssen has over fifteen years of recruiting experience. He holds a bachelor's degree in human resource management and an MBA with a concentration in human resource management, and he is a certified personnel consultant.

CPSIA information can be obtained
at www.ICGtesting.com
Printed in the USA
FSHW04n0327170418
47067FS